Bundle of Joy

*A Devotional to Accompany
Your Child's Diagnosis*

MELANIE GOMEZ

Copyright © 2017 Melanie Gomez
All rights reserved.

ISBN: 1544255004
ISBN 13: 9781544255002

This book is dedicated to you, reader. I've come to discover that all the wonderful things that God has shown me, and allowed me to experience so joyfully, have a purpose. That purpose is to encourage other special-needs moms on their journey: to be a lighthouse up ahead that shines brightly and leads away from the darkness of fear, disappointment, stress, and sorrow. Then, my dear, it will be your turn to lead others.

CONTENTS

Acknowledgments		vii
Introduction		ix
Part 1	Our Story	1
Part 2	Devotionals	11
1	Perspective	13
2	Fear	16
3	Strength	19
4	Peace	22
5	Courage	25
6	Hope	28
7	Perseverance	31
8	Purpose	34
9	Why?	37
10	Goodness	40
11	Transformation	43
12	Finish	46
13	Praise	48
14	Choose	51
About the Author		55

ACKNOWLEDGMENTS

Thank you, dear Tony, for supporting and encouraging this project. A very rare gem are you, to be so wonderful throughout this whole process. I love and appreciate you, and not a moment of your cheerleading for me has gone unnoticed. You are my rock.

Thank you, dear Benjamin, for being the world's best son. What would I do without your grace, forgiveness, and patience to counterbalance the challenges of raising a special child? God has such huge plans for you that I cannot fathom, but I know they are established on the fact that you are, and have, an exceptional brother.

Thank you, dear Nicolas, for opening my eyes to a whole new world, for pushing me into God, where I experienced the true meaning of perfection and love.

Thank you to my sister and my parents, for raising a strong girl without fears or doubts. I may have never started this journey without the heritage you passed on to me.

Thank you, God, for sending Jesus to redeem me, to awaken me from a hopeless slumber to a glorious life in you and for you. What an awesome and profound love you lavish on us.

INTRODUCTION

I pray that the eyes of your heart may be enlightened in order that you may know the hope to which he has called you, the riches of his glorious inheritance in his holy people and his incomparably great power for us who believe.

—*Ephesians 1:18 (NIV)*

Every mom has unique challenges. I'm convinced each of us find ourselves completely alone at times, in situations unlike those faced by any other. However, there is a *special* motherhood path that is not the one commonly taken. The moment a child receives a diagnosis of special needs, the parents are forever special as well. This doesn't mean we can't be counted as normal people, but it does mean we are also numbered among the exceptional. I have two boys; one fits within the boundaries of typical health and development, and the other was diagnosed with a genetic disorder when he was six months old. Both are extraordinary, both have required me to stretch my faith, and both are precious gifts from my loving Father God. But there is something about my journey as a special mom that has completely altered every facet of my life. I credit that journey with causing me to question, unravel, and examine everything that I am—and thereafter to put it all back together in a new, almost unrecognizable way and make me a person filled with passion and purpose as I never was before.

The special experiences in my life have been so life-changing and overwhelming that they have revealed a light and truth that were completely hidden from my view. It is for the purpose of pulling back this curtain that I write. The eyes of my heart—what I see not in the natural, but in the grand scheme of life and eternity—have been enlightened. I write so that another mom can encounter the same enlightenment and truth.

If you are looking at this text now, you most likely have recently been pointed down the path less traveled, the path most of us would never voluntarily choose: being a parent of a child with special needs. I don't know what the future holds or what the doctors have predicted, but I do know a few things: (1) you don't really have time to read a book; (2) you now love your child with a fierce, fiery love that no one can fathom; and (3) you don't possess the strength, courage, or expertise to do this on your own.

My hope is that you will carve out little niches of time to read. There is no right or wrong way to go through this book. You can start at the beginning with our diagnosis story, a sort-of introduction to me and my journey. You can also jump to the devotional section first and then go back and get to know me later on. However you arrive at the devotionals, read one per day, or per week, or just read the same one over and over until it sinks in. Sometimes a momma's bruised heart is hardened, and it takes a while for us to allow something new to penetrate down deep. I don't want to take your time away from your baby or your busy life, but I am asking you to give a little bit of your time to God. Your heavenly Father is anxiously waiting to reveal things to you, things that will take some time to hear, see, and know.

Enjoy reading his word and his truth, and hopefully my explanation of it from a special mom's perspective will help it accomplish its purpose for you in this season. I look forward to sitting with you over these next few pages while you see, with new eyes, the precious gift you hold in your bundle of joy.

PART 1

Our Story

Each of us will experience only one moment—or at the most a handful of moments—that are truly life-changing. Although that phrase is often thrown around about things like desserts or spa days, an event that redirects every moment for the rest of your life is unforgettable. My husband, Tony, and I experienced our life-changing moment sixteen years ago.

My second pregnancy was as typical as the first, and I loved being pregnant. When our precious Nicolas was born, he was the completion of a perfect family. A little brother for three-year-old Benjamin and a second son made everything seem neatly rounded out. Although he was a little smaller and was born with a few small hitches, he was the crowning addition to our family, and we joyfully took him home to continue building our lives with two rowdy, messy, momma-loving little boys rather than one.

Unlike my firstborn, Nicolas required a few follow-up appointments after the hospital—"no big deal," normal things that happen sometimes with babies. At birth, Nicolas had an umbilical hernia, "hip clicks," and a tiny hole in his heart. The first specialist we ever visited was a sweet and highly respected pediatric cardiologist who ran tests and explained that this was fairly common. She explained that if the hole did not resolve on its own, she could fix it surgically—no big deal, she does it all the time, and the babies all live happily ever after. *OK*, I thought. *This is a little trial that we must endure, but in the end everything will be perfect, and we'll be fine.* I consider myself a very strong person, and I was proud to be able to persevere through this potential crisis as a calm and steady rock for my family. We followed up with monthly tests, and eventually the hole closed itself, but the chapter on our baby's complications did not close.

Even the healthiest of newborns requires pediatric checkups. During one or two of those weekly visits, I mentioned that I noticed Nicolas making a lot of gurgles and choking noises while he slept. After the doctor dismissed it the first time or two, we were eventually referred to a pediatric gastroenterologist. The second of our new list of pediatric specialists dispatched us to the radiology department on suspicion of reflux. By the end of an afternoon that had started with a routine "well-baby checkup," I was told that my Nicolas, the one with the tiny hole in his heart, had an intestinal malrotation that should be surgically corrected. The surgeon explained the entire process, anesthesia and all, and tears ran down my cheeks even while I was determined to remain strong. I was proud to once again persevere through this bump in the road, and

I was confident we'd come through just fine and live happily ever after.

Nicolas underwent intestinal surgery at three months old, on the day of big brother Benjamin's third birthday, September 11. His recovery was swift, and in a few days, we were back on our way to normal. I wore the successful outcome and perseverance like a badge of honor: "I can weather any storm," I proudly concluded about myself.

As Nicolas approached four months of age, the cardiologist reported that the hole in his heart had closed on its own—miracle of miracles—and surgery would not be required. Simultaneous with this positive news, I became slightly unnerved by the distinct contrasts I noticed between Nicolas and Benjamin. I began poring over Ben's baby book of milestones, as well as all the parenting books and developmental charts I could find, to try and put my finger on what was so different about Nicolas. I mentioned my concerns to the pediatrician, who scolded me for committing that motherly "mistake" of comparing my children. "No two babies are the same," she reminded me. I knew that, of course, as I'd been studying baby books every moment that I wasn't nursing or sleeping.

Another week went by, and I was more convinced that something wasn't right—again, the pediatrician sent me back home. My brave, strong persona was still intact, so I worked very hard to hide my fears and suspicions. But during a moment of weakness, I confessed to my husband that although the doctors were sure Nicolas was fine, I was certain that he was not. The next morning my dear hubby was on the phone with the pediatrician, who set up a referral visit with a neurologist—not because something was wrong, but they contrived that it was the only way to help me feel better and rule out, once and for all, any problems with our baby.

The neurologist was our third pediatric specialist. Both previous experiences with this type of visit had brought difficult news, but they had been issues that were now completely resolved, so our spirits were high. The doctor looked at Nicolas, ran all the neurological tests one can run on a four-and-a-half-month-old infant, and determined that there was probably nothing wrong. However, he explained, "The brain is like a computer. Sometimes when there are lots of small, seemingly unrelated glitches, it can be an indication of a problem in the programming." I experienced the concurrent emotions of both relief and alarm that my concerns may be valid. He referred us to a geneticist who would help us rule out anything serious; he was fairly sure that Nicolas was fine.

Next stop: the geneticist, our fourth specialist. She was also very kind and fairly certain that Nicolas did not have any genetic disorder. She explained she'd been doing this long enough that she could usually tell by observation. However, she prescribed full genetic testing for him—another rule-out scenario.

Between all the specialists' visits, there were a plethora of tests—MRI, EEGs, EKGs, blood screens—tests with sedation, restraints, monitors, and more specialists. During all of this, my strong, courageous front was being constantly assaulted. I maintained my calm composure, but at an ever-increasing price of sleepless nights and a thick cloud around my heart during the day. The tests were all simple, yet the process of each was terribly distressing. IVs and blood draws on infant arms are excruciating to witness; sedation was temporary but had disquieting side effects. And the vision of your infant wrapped in wires, tubes, and hospital gowns is dreadful. I became uncomfortably familiar with the local children's hospital. We had agreed not to tell our family and friends any of these developments because, as the specialists had assured us, it was probably nothing. I was desperate for all this to end so we could get back to our normal lives.

Finally the appointment arrived where we would learn the results of the genetic testing, rule out anything too serious, and move on. My husband and I sat together with our chubby baby boy in anticipation. The doctor was very kind as she explained very slowly in detail how chromosomes are engineered and how, in Nicolas's case and much to her surprise, the slight variation of one of them had occurred. Each segment of every unique chromosome is responsible for different details that constitute who we are. In Nicolas's case, the "p" segment of chromosome 8 was duplicated on top of itself, and the tip was deleted. That's the moment that my heart lost all strength.

The geneticist handed us a medical journal article with a study of individuals with this particular syndrome. It was a fairly rare disorder, and the most accurate prognosis she could provide was this recent research conducted on five individuals with the same genetic pattern. I began to peruse the pages, and although she kept talking, I didn't hear anything else she said. I saw words like "severe mental retardation"; descriptions of heart and kidney problems, absent speech, common surgeries, and severe orthopedic problems; and photographs of disfigured children's faces. I kept my usual strong, composed posture through the rest of the visit but heard nothing else. My husband listened and latched onto her disclaimer that each case is different, and just because certain symptoms may be listed in the journal finding, they weren't guaranteed for Nicolas—his case would be unique to him. I vaguely remember that she suggested having more children so that Nicolas would have plenty of siblings to help care for him as we aged. One of the few words I heard her mention reverberated in my head as the connotations and derogatory definitions, along with childhood memories of strange faces and behaviors, swirled in my mind: "special."

I don't know what exactly my husband and I spoke of as we left that office. Such a heavy weight had just been handed to us in a single moment. I remember that he seemed much more optimistic than I was, and that was irritating to me. I categorized him as "in denial," and as he drove away to work, I secured the baby in his infant seat, climbed into my car, and cried. And cried. There weren't words that could fully express my emotions. In just a moment, I felt the defeat of every aspiration, dream, and hope a mother's heart has for her child. The devastation in my heart mingled with the overwhelming flood of love and forceful protectiveness I felt, as I looked at the precious baby in the seat next to me. One whom I always loved as special was now defined by that word in an entirely different way.

Thus far in this process, my faith and hope in God had remained firm. I was born and raised in the church, and since my first baby was born, I'd had a renewed sense of God's importance and protection in my life. Over the previous six to eight weeks, I was confident that God had heard my prayers, and the doctors' reports would all be positive. Although my instinct, while I drove away, was to pray, I found neither the desire to communicate with God nor the words to speak. At the same time, based on what that journal article said, my gut knew that God was our only chance.

That moment occurred sixteen years ago. It was not the end of my story, dear friend, only the beginning. Through these years our family of four has experienced a journey that has been exciting and challenging, joy-filled and sometimes sad, and always overflowing with love. Nicolas is the light of our lives. He's also the light of the lives of many others outside of our foursome. Nicolas struggles, yes. He still doesn't read or write or express himself completely; he is not independent. But he has miraculously exceeded many of his diagnosis expectations. It's important to point out that something amazing happened somewhere between that journal article of dreadful prognosis and real life with a special child. Only by the grace of God have my eyes been opened to see the truth of our story and the full perspective of our lives. That article didn't mention any of the ways that one actually quantifies quality of life: Joy—Nick is loaded with it, and it's contagious. Purity—his heart always believes and hopes for the best. Love—Nick is more loving and affectionate than anyone I've ever met. When I tally the "haves" and "have-nots," Nicolas comes out far ahead, as do all whose lives he has touched and forever changed. He was a complicated little bundle, for sure, but in totality a bundle of joy from beginning to end.

PART 2

Devotionals

1

PERSPECTIVE

*As the heavens are higher than the earth,
so are my ways higher than your ways and
my thoughts than your thoughts.*

—*Isaiah 55:9(NIV)*

As I held a genetic diagnosis printout in my hand, there were a lot of facts staring back at me. What I saw pointed in a very specific direction: a life of fear, disappointment, stress, and sorrow were all that my eyes could see. For weeks, months, and years I looked over and over at that diagnosis. I didn't need to pull the paper out of the drawer anymore; it was all engraved in my mind's eye. All the while God waited patiently to show me something else. He nudged me repeatedly to stop looking at those words on paper and to refocus my eyes. God does not see what we see. Our perspective through human eyes is so limited, flawed, and filtered that we should not ever rely on our eyes, thoughts, or logic. It took me a while to stop using my own limited sight and allow God the opportunity to show me his perspective.

This revelation hit me while reading a much bigger story than mine, in the book of Exodus.

This story begins in Exodus 3, where we find Moses walking through the desert. Moses is contentedly living life in anonymity, shepherding a flock of sheep under the afternoon sun, when he sees in the distance a burning bush. As he walks toward the bush to get a closer look, God's voice audibly calls him by name: "Moses!" And when Moses replies, "Here am I," the voice says: "Do not come any closer. Take off your sandals, for the place where you are standing is holy ground" (Ex 3:5).

The conversation continues, but I camped out right here. Most of the time in reading this story, we focus on the awesomeness of a burning bush. But to create such a spectacle, God must have had a really important message to deliver, and I believe that every single word of it is crucial.

The very first instruction: Moses had to take off his sandals and become barefoot. The sand on which he stood was identical to the sand that he had been walking on—there was no visible difference. This is an epic demonstration of the difference between God's perspective and our own. God is saying and showing, before anything else, that he does not see things the way we see them. God sees a completely different reality from ours: the next bit of sand, which would look, feel, smell, and even taste the same to Moses, is completely different, and God is asking Moses to take his word for it. Was

God speaking figuratively? No! The truth is that our limited, flawed human perspective does not compare to God's perfect, omnipotent vision. So God's opening sentence, in a conversation to present Moses his destiny, high purpose, and the future of God's people, is about perspective.

The diagnosis the geneticist gave my precious six-month-old son didn't look good. I could see no way that this was anything other than utter disaster, failure, and disappointment at the very highest level. I was looking at this prognosis and my son's impending struggles with my own eyes, with my own worldly knowledge of disability. It took me years to understand this basic fact: God does not see my son as I see my son. He does not define success or failure by the same standards that the world uses. He has a specific purpose and destiny for each of us, and as we live out that purpose, we achieve success in his kingdom. The world sees my son as flawed, but God sees him as knit together perfectly to accomplish his destiny. The more we intentionally shut off our own thoughts, fears, worries, stress, and hyperfocus on the negative we see, the more God will graciously and lovingly reveal the beauty, wholeness, joy, and positives he sees in the same situation.

> *Lean in: Take just one moment to acknowledge that your heavenly Father sees things you don't. It's OK to tell him you don't get it—I confessed that to him so many times! Ask him to show you, and he will. Each day meditate on the truth that he has a way and a perfect plan for you and your child.*

2

FEAR

*For God has not given us a spirit of fear, but
of power and of love and of a sound mind.*

—*2 Timothy 1:7 (NKJV)*

Fear was one of the greatest weights I carried with me at the beginning of this journey. There were so many uncertainties that my mind could become overwhelmed with a foggy dread that hovered over my thoughts and actions. If I were to consciously think about the what-ifs of the future, it would send me into a dark, fearful place. But even when I wasn't intentionally dwelling on those things, my subconscious always had a little storm cloud looming nearby.

I don't know if I recognized it as fear—I think I rationalized it as commonsense concern, my "mom brain" functioning cautiously, as intended. When he was still little, I could lie awake at night, gripped by fear about what would happen when his father and I were too old to care for him or when we passed away before him. I feared even the tiniest of things; I remember that I was almost paralyzed by fear when he rode his first rollercoaster. But somewhere along the lines, I learned a valuable lesson that freed me mentally, spiritually, and emotionally more than any other. It was that no matter what happens, or what had already happened, God is still God. God is, was, and will be. No one is guaranteed anything in the future—so then fear of the future becomes meaningless. I justified my fear, because my child's future was uncertain; then I realized: so is everyone's! I also realized that God promises to work all things out for our good—how can I fear that?

Mostly, the above verse tells me that fear, no matter how much it makes sense to our human minds, is not from God. He purposefully endowed us with access to his spirit, with power, love, and a sound mind. Not fear. So I simply had to dwell on those things—become conscious of the power, love, and soundness of mind that were at my disposal—and the fear would go. I could defeat those fearful thoughts each time by telling myself that I was filled with power and love and that my mind was sound. The sound mind in this verse is also translated as "self-discipline" and "self-control" in other Bible translations. That means that God has given me the ability to shut down the fearful thoughts that aren't from him.

On the topic of fear, I recently came across this passage in a wonderful book I'm reading called *Undaunted*, by Christine Caine:

> As long as you live you will have something to lose—little pieces of yourself…there is always some cause for fear. We can choose to surrender to that fear and let it rule our lives, or we can surrender to Christ all of those things we love and fear to lose, and then live fearlessly—undaunted.

By surrendering my son and his future back to God, I release all the fear that goes with it. I say "back to God" because I acknowledge that God is the source of my life, my children, and our family. He allows me to influence and manage all that he gifted me with, but he ultimately is the author and finisher; so I put back in his hands what came from his hands.

> *Lean in: What is it that you fear the most for yourself or your child? Today, know that your fear, no matter how well founded, is not from God. He has given you access to a sound mind and courage as you walk through that situation. Ask him to deposit his spirit and love in your mind so that all fear is driven out.*

3

STRENGTH

I pray that out of his glorious riches he may strengthen you with power through his Spirit in your inner being.

—*Ephesians 3:16 (NIV)*

Probably the one thing that I have lacked most often during my life as a special mom is strength. You wouldn't know it, because I have a strong demeanor. I typically appear unshaken by what the world throws at me and unmoved by disappointment or setbacks. I'm not a basket case or a bundle of nerves. But there have been days since my baby's diagnosis when I have felt so very weak. My "inner being" is like a deflated balloon or a bowl full of warm Jell-O.

In Ephesians 3, Paul is not referring to physical strength. He is encouraging his friends to have the strength to remain in Christ. This is the strength and power to comprehend and then faithfully remember the depth of Christ's love for us. That is the supernatural power that is required when we are weak on the inside. The apostle writes of something that often goes unmentioned and unacknowledged. There is a great depth of weakness that can occur on the inside, while the outside keeps up appearances. There are times when it feels like keeping our faith intact is too hard. Carrying on as if there is a good God who is looking down on me lovingly, watching over me, and blessing me…sometimes I feel as though I may not have the fortitude it takes to keep that up. That's OK. It's the reason for Paul's prayer for the Ephesians. Thank God we have this letter so that we know we are not alone; our generation is not the first to deal with such weakness. Ephesians 3:16 is what we have as a help so that we can buck up and regain the strength we need. This promise is what I can read every single morning and know that if I simply close my eyes and ask for strength and power, the Lord will renew and refresh me. I have found supernatural strength in the midst of the darkest moments, not on my own, but by recalling this one promise. Feelings of weakness and defeat are things that will definitely come calling over and over. It will also be easier to defeat, each time, the sooner we remember that we have a promise of strength and power for our inner being that cannot be defeated, shut down, or overcome. God's glorious riches are more than enough fuel for my spirit, and they are available to me at all times.

> *Lean in: Are your emotions convincing you of a different story? Read Ephesians 3:16–19 aloud to yourself. Tell*

your emotions they don't get the final say today; rather, God's Spirit in your inner being will be in charge of your mind and heart today. That is the place where, when all else is weak, you have glorious riches of strength. Tap into that strength and find the power you require.

4

PEACE

[A]nd the peace of God, which transcends all understanding, will guard your hearts and your minds through Christ Jesus.

—Philippians 4:7 (NIV)

"Peace that surpasses all understanding" is one of the sweetest gifts that I know. During the initial days, months, and years of my son's diagnosis, peace was elusive. I knew *of* it, but it escaped my efforts to hold it permanently in my heart or mind. Even the sweetest moment that *felt* peaceful—a sleeping infant at my bosom or a smiling, chubby face—would be overtaken by a flood of tears and sorrow. My mind would mock itself for feeling at peace, when it knew better.

Nevertheless, it is a solid promise that we are all guaranteed if we are saved through Christ. So how on earth does a special mom overcome the "facts" that her mind knows backward and forward to achieve peace in the storm?

Check out this translation of Philippians 4:7 in the Amplified Bible:

> [A]nd God's peace [shall be yours, that tranquil state of a soul assured of its salvation through Christ, and so fearing nothing from God and being content with its earthly lot of whatever sort that is, that peace] which transcends all understanding shall garrison and mount guard over your hearts and minds in Christ Jesus.

You may have noticed that the verse is the second half of a sentence. The first part of the sentence says this: "Do not fret or have any anxiety about anything, but in every circumstance and in everything, by prayer and petition, with thanksgiving, continue to make your wants known to God." Tell him everything. All of it. Then the peace arrives. When I take it all to God in prayer, withholding nothing and being completely transparent about everything, I unfurl it all to his loving, compassionate ear. And then, after it all goes out to him, a wonderful peace comes in and floods all the space that was once taken up by worry. I love the end of the amplified version that says the peace will mount a guard over my heart and mind. Once that peace is in place, fear, anxiety, and worry will have a much harder time coming back in. The Message version says, "Let petitions and praises shape your worries into prayers."

Peace is life-changing. Without a doubt it is the single factor that makes me a different person now than when we first received the diagnosis. It has become an almost mysterious quality about me that is my witness to others on a daily basis more than anything else I do or say. It is something that I very specifically and intentionally have prayed for many, many times. Like a favorite piece of jewelry, it became the gift I put on each day before I got out of bed. You may be in the place where confessing all your fears, anger, disappointment, and stress feels wrong. But the only way to achieve peace is to be honest with God—honest about everything and anything. The Message version of the verses concludes this way: "[A] sense of God's wholeness, everything coming together for good, will come and settle you down. It's wonderful what happens when Christ displaces worry at the center of your life."

> *Lean in: Would being completely honest with God seem wrong? Do you feel like it would make you a bad mom to confess the depths of your fear, disappointment, stress, or sorrow? It's not, and it doesn't. I promise. Your heavenly Father already knows and is lovingly waiting for you to give it all to him, place it at his feet, and allow his* peace *to begin to displace it all.*

5

COURAGE

I will go before you and will level the mountains; I will break down gates of bronze and cut through bars of iron. I will give you hidden treasures, riches stored in secret places, so that you may know that I am the Lord, the God of Israel, who summons you by name.

—Isaiah 45:2–4(NIV)

He *is* there already, was there first, in this strange new land. This is a promise of the Lord to us who believe. He is our loving Father who would not put us in a place he did not know. It reminds me of when I visited daycares for my firstborn son. I went there so many times, sat in the room, and studied the ladies and what they did, how they interacted with the babies. I knew exactly where I was sending my precious child, even the tiniest detail, before I ever left him there alone. He was fifteen weeks old and had no way of knowing all that. I knew that on his first day, he would just wake up and see a different crib than he had ever known, hear different noises, and be held by different hands with different smells...I am sure that was all so frightening for him, and his baby brain couldn't do anything but cry itself to sleep. But I *knew* where he was; he was safe, it was part of the plan, and I had been there before him. I had taken his favorite toys and blankets from home, and soon enough he figured it out.

On the days when we have enough strength to lift our eyes and peer down the road of where our special path is leading, what do we see? Mountains? Iron bars? Closed and locked doors? The Bible promises that God will not only be with us but will go before us. He levels mountains before we get to them. We just have to keep going. My first instinct when I see the mountain is to stop. Just camp out here; it's gonna get harder because I can see right up ahead that the road will get steep, and I'll have to climb uphill. Or will I? Each time I have viewed something that, in my own perspective, looks like it's too difficult to continue, the Lord has been faithful to cut through the iron bars before I get there. Whether a physical challenge, developmental roadblock, or other obstacle, I have found that if I just keep going with faith in the one who will level the mountains, I am able to persevere and reach the other side. I don't ever stop learning this lesson as a special mom. Every time we get to the other side of one mountain, there is another.

Because this scenario recurs so often, I am now able to push through much more quickly and easily—mostly because of the end of the above verse: not only am I promised that he has gone before me but also that he will give me hidden treasures. Each time our path "reroutes" or an obstacle is traversed, there is a sweet new treasure. Maybe it's a new relationship, a new skill for my guy, or a new deep heart change for me. I promise that we can count on this one thing: When we keep going and trust that God is there before us, there will be riches awaiting us in that secret place that lies just on the other side. We will always come through and look back to say "Yes! I know that he is the Lord."

> *Lean in: Where is the place or situation where you need the Lord to level the mountains and break down the gates? Spend time today simply thanking God that he is in that place ahead of you. Whatever the situation, he is there—now—and will make a way for you. Believe that you will sense his presence and uncover the hidden treasures that are stored therein. Ask him to show you and to give you the confidence to believe his promise in Isaiah 45:2–4.*

6

HOPE

We have this hope as an anchor for the soul, firm and secure. It enters the inner sanctuary behind the curtain, where our forerunner, Jesus, has entered on our behalf. He has become a high priest forever.

—Hebrews 6:19–20a (NIV)

"For I know the plans I have for you," declares the Lord, "plans to prosper you and not to harm you, plans to give you hope and a future.

—Jeremiah 29:11(NIV)

The most comforting thought I have experienced is that God's plan for my life is to give me hope and a future. Lots of people quote Jeremiah 29:11 because of its promise of prosperity or protection. I must say that as a mom whose baby's future is so uncertain, hope is that one thing I can't do without. There are days of setbacks and challenges when I can't imagine one good reason to get out of bed! Hebrew 6:19–20 says, "*But* we have this hope as an anchor for the soul, firm and secure. It enters the inner sanctuary behind the curtain, where our forerunner, Jesus, has entered on our behalf." I emphasize the word "but" there because it is actually one of my favorite words in the Bible (super weird, let me explain).

I love how the authors of the Bible used that little conjunction over and over again: they spell out a dire situation, a negative prognosis, a disaster waiting to happen, and then they write my favorite three letters, "but." Everyone from David to Queen Esther to the New Testament apostles had their "but" moments. I like to think of having hope as always having a "but." Praise the Lord; I can recite endless stories of how things looked bad, *but God*. Let me make it clear that this applies to every area of our life. Having a special baby affects everything. The ripple effect of a diagnosis rocks it all. Some of my "buts" include:

- My marriage was almost over, but God redeemed it.
- Our financial crisis was about to drown us, but God made a way for us to overcome.
- And, of course, my child was given a life sentence of despair, but God substituted it for a life filled with joy.

Because all things work together for the good of those who love God, our marriage crisis actually made us so much stronger. The financial crisis pushed us to Biblical financial wisdom that changed our future. The genetic disorder that should have stolen my child actually gave me one who was more than wonderful.

There is always hope in Jesus, because we are guaranteed that every situation has a "but"! There is an anchor for my soul, which makes it firm and secure. Jesus is my high priest forever, which means he is my perpetual "way where there is no way"; he is always the answer to every unknown. He covers me, provides for me, and intercedes for me in advance before I am ever even aware of a need.

> *Lean in: Whatever you are facing today, try writing it down or saying it out loud, not with a period at the end of the sentence, but rather conclude with these three letters and a few leading, promising, hopeful dots: but…*

7

PERSEVERANCE

*And let us run with perseverance the race
marked out for us, fixing our eyes on Jesus,
the pioneer and perfecter of faith.*

—*Hebrews 12:1b–2a (NIV)*

I grew up singing this old gospel song on Sunday mornings: "Turn your eyes upon Jesus, look full in his wonderful face. And the things of earth will grow strangely dim, in the light of his glory and grace." I had no idea what it meant. I figured it out only recently.

Through the early months and years of having a special baby, I became aware that a perspective shift was key. But it took much longer to realize that the change of perspective I had been working toward was more than a shift in how I perceived a circumstance or situation; actually, I was shifting my focus to look upon something else entirely…to be specific, Jesus. When your mind's eye switches its focus to Christ, it cannot see any situation negatively.

The ultimate result of my change in this journey is a redefinition of the word "special." It reminds me of a passage from Paul's letter to Titus in verse 1:15, which says that to the pure, all things are pure. The word "special," in the most pure form, means something extraordinary and to be highly valued. The rest of the verse says, "But to those who are defiled and unbelieving, nothing is pure. Both their mind and conscience are defiled." The meaning of special had been tainted in my own mind. Since I was young I knew that special, as referring to individuals who were different, really meant "less than"—not highly valued. Not something extraordinary, but something oddball and abnormal. My own thoughts had been defiled and were working against me to shut out the truth of God and replace it with the perspective of society. I was unbelieving, and therefore my mind and conscience were unavailable to receive truth and purity.

I realize now that Nicolas is very special. He is a unique, extraordinary gift. It's not sugarcoating. It's not saying nice things or thinking positive thoughts in order to disguise the truth. It is *the* truth. There is no way I would be able to "see" that if I were simply to look with my eyes upon the natural evidence of Nicolas. Looking at physical limitations, cognitive deficits, and other weaknesses with basic human reasoning, one would not perceive "special." However, when I focus on Christ—his love, his salvation, his perfection—I perceive the overwhelming specialness of his plan and provision for my life, including—no, especially—Nicolas.

> *Lean in: Rather than striving to see something differently, why not try to just stop looking at that thing or situation entirely. As the song suggests, allow it to grow strangely dim in the light of Christ's glory and grace. Focus on how completely enveloped in God's mercy you are today, how he alone is the author and finisher of your life and how he alone is the one who can mend broken hearts and redeem lost dreams.*

8

PURPOSE

*And who knows but that you have come to
your royal position for such a time as this?*

—*Esther 4:14b (NIV)*

Life as a special-needs mom is about as far away from royalty as you can get! Remarkably, however, I have found great wisdom within Esther's pages. How on earth could I identify with a queen? Well, first of all, Esther wasn't born a queen. She started out as a regular girl with a less-than-glamorous and even less-than-average life. Then she kept running into extremely unlikely circumstances. Every step of her journey was completely atypical for someone like her. (Sounds more familiar now, right?) Yet God designed each of those steps specifically for a great purpose she could have never fathomed.

It was out of the realm of possibility that God would take her on this journey to save her people—her people weren't even in danger at the time her unique, lonely process began. Yet there she was, alone and unlike anyone else around her. She was in a role that she didn't want or enjoy, and I imagine she often thought, *Lord, you've picked the wrong girl for this!* OK, so now that you see how eerily similar you and I are to Queen Esther, let's look at the inspiration she can provide.

The Bible says that each of us is born with a specific destiny and purpose. God designs us—both our inner workings and our external experiences—to achieve our unique destiny. He knows that whatever you're going through right now is a crucial element to your fulfillment, which is why he allows it to be part of you. So don't reject it, don't despise it, and don't wish it were for someone else…it's not part of that other person's destiny; it's yours. Once we embrace that it is intended for our good, we can see it differently and start living like Esther: in a royal position for such a time as this! No, your sweat pants and T-shirt won't magically transform into a ball gown upon this realization, but your mind, your attitude, and even your countenance will change. You will seem more regal, more "on purpose," and you will then be well on your way to walking toward that destiny.

I can promise from experience that every single thing that has happened in your life, no matter what it was—painful, joyful, regrettable, forgettable—has been integral in the making of Royal You. Never regret anything that led to now! Never fear what you're about to go through, because it will lead to something new! If you read the whole book of Esther, you'll see that she couldn't have known her destiny was to save her people from extinction, because that threat didn't exist at the time that she was ripped away from her life and thrown into chaos and uncertainty. I was not a writer, not a speaker, not an encourager, and not even much of a friend when I became a special-needs mom who knew nothing and regretted everything! I couldn't have known what my destiny was because I didn't even know such a thing existed. But now, living in the aftermath, I feel fulfilled, called, and driven like never before. I feel "on purpose" in so many ways.

You, too, have come to your position for such a time as this, my friend! It may not make sense now, but that's OK. Just because the final purpose isn't clearly visible, never doubt that God has a plan.

> *Lean in: Take a few moments to look back over your life and what has brought you to this place today. Ask God to show you his design and pattern within your history, whether good, bad, or ugly. Your unique journey has brought you to this time and this day for a purpose. Gaining a greater understanding of your purpose, and your child's purpose, can heal and restore places that you thought were wastelands. Dreams that you thought were dead can come alive again within his divine purpose for your life. As you move forward, knowing that his design continues to unfold will remind you to trust him.*

9

WHY?

*[I]n the hope of eternal life, which God, who does
not lie, promised before the beginning of time.*

—*Titus 1:2 (NIV)*

Why did this happen? That is the honest and very uncomfortable question. It is the biggest obstacle to surrender. When my baby was diagnosed with a genetic disorder and given a prognosis of lifetime struggles and hardship, I blamed God. I was really angry with him. "Why?" screamed louder than my ability to hear an answer. I am going to show you what I believe is the biblical, scriptural truth about a very sensitive, misunderstood subject, which is this: God doesn't cause suffering. He does not inflict illness, loss, or tragedy on people. It is important for you to know in your heart of hearts that God doesn't kill children, put cancer in bodies, cause airplanes to crash, or any of the other things we may have heard attributed to him. I have heard people say, "God needed another angel in heaven, so he took your baby," or "God took him too soon," or any number of variations on those themes. It may appease the grief-stricken mind at first, but I imagine it can easily become a seed of disdain and anger that will fester and grow toward a God who would act so cruelly.

Since Jesus came into the world and paid every debt of sin that we owe, there is now no cause for God to inflict punishment. God does not seek our destruction. The Bible states that there is one who "prowls around like a roaring lion looking for someone to devour" (1 Pt 5:8). And because of that one, Satan, there are many times each day, all over the world, where he wreaks havoc in the hopes of devouring his prey. The Bible also shows us examples of when God allows Satan to have his way, so that God can use the situation for a greater good.

My point is that in order to truly believe, have hope, and achieve peace, our heart must settle on this: There is one great "I AM" who does not cause suffering, disease, or disaster. He loves us, and he has a plan for us that includes joy, peace, love, and fulfillment. God, in his infinite wisdom and love for us, may allow Satan to perpetrate something that we don't understand, because God knows that it will actually become a blessing in disguise, and it can be a seed of something far greater than we could imagine.

> *Lean in: Does any part of you blame God? Or have you believed that somehow this was punishment from*

him? Today look at your current crisis as Satan's attempt to derail your life and your future. See that God is with you, loves you, and can see a happy ending for your life in spite of it—most probably because of it. Trust that he knows that without this challenge, the ultimate destiny of you, your child, and others would not be fulfilled. Believe today that he didn't do it, but he allowed it for your good. Will you now allow him to use it to heal you?

10

GOODNESS

*I would have lost heart, unless I had believed that I would
see the goodness of the LORD in the land of the living.*

—*Psalms 27:13 (NKJV)*

Losing heart. This is the deathblow to your spirit. It's giving up all hope and surrendering completely to disappointment and despair. Oh, how often that has loomed close at my doorstep! I wish I could say the only time was after our initial diagnosis. But the truth is that over these past sixteen years, the possibility of losing heart has felt imminent on a number of occasions—sometimes during a crisis, other times during a walk in the park watching typical children my son's age interact and be "normal." I am in good company to know that even the psalmist was teetering on the brink of losing heart at times. I can also be encouraged by his reason that he did not lose heart. No matter where I find myself, no matter how dark or desperate the situation seems, I can remind myself that I *will* see the goodness of God in this lifetime.

Within Psalm 23, which I memorized as a child, there is a phrase that I never fully comprehended: walking through the valley of the shadow of death. It wasn't until I was faced with loss that I understood what the valley was—being overshadowed by death, but not dying. If I am alive, I can continue to walk through the shadow of death, because I know that a valley, by definition, has an end where I will start to go up and over the next mountain. I may be overshadowed by the death of hopes or dreams, or even loved ones, but I live. And because I still live, I have some tiny spark of hope that remains, even if I do not sense it.

My life today is a testament to the goodness of God in this land of the living. How? Because I did not lose heart completely, I was able to continue on. The goodness of God was not at first evident. But it is promised to arrive in the here and now, not just in heaven after we leave this earth. The further I go, the more I see his goodness. Particularly I see it in my child with special needs. How amazing is it that the qualities of an omnipotent, omniscient God can be most vividly seen within the weakest and most limited humans? Glimpsing God's goodness is what it takes to keep our heads above water just a little longer, because we know the floodwaters will recede, and the promise will be fulfilled.

Lean in: Can you step back just far enough from your current situation to believe in God's goodness? Whatever depth your heart may sink to, let it not be lost. Believe that his goodness will be seen by you, during your lifetime. Believing that takes expectation. Begin to expect and prepare for that day. It is coming!

11

TRANSFORMATION

Do not conform to the pattern of this world, but be transformed by the renewing of your mind. Then you will be able to test and approve what God's will is—His good, pleasing and perfect will.

—Romans 12:2 (NIV)

Unfortunately, seeing with a new perspective is not like surgically replacing our eyes with God's; it's not even like wearing new glasses. We don't just acquire a new perspective, after which point the old is gone, never to return. It is much more like any new (and difficult) skill that must be practiced continually, using muscles in new and awkward ways. It is the continuous "renewing of the mind" to which we are encouraged in Romans 12:2. Daily renewal of the mind, no matter how specific or unique your life or situation, is exactly the same for everyone. It is daily acknowledging that the only way to "know" anything true is to surrender my perspective, plans, and will for God's. The more I seek him, the clearer my perspective becomes. Eventually I don't see perspective; I see only him. I even lay down the deep desire to understand something. That is the final layer of surrender, and it truly is a daily (sometimes hourly) pursuit. This is where we all see that no matter how extraordinary or unique our story is, it has a simple solution. Actually, it doesn't get any more simple. Easy, no. But simple all the same. Wake up, hand it all over to God, go through the day reminding yourself that it's all his, and go to sleep at night knowing that it's all his. Repeat.

Part two of this verse is the reason for a renewed mind: to know God's good, pleasing, and perfect will. That's what I want to see. That's the view that a perspective shift provides. I believe this verse confirms that without a daily renewal of the mind, permanent change is impossible. I did not know what "perfect" truly was until my mind was renewed and my perspective adjusted. I can easily fall back into my old habits and ways of thinking unless I am renewed daily. The old perspective is right there, over a steep cliff edge that has no railing. That tumble back into seeing with my own perspective always results in disappointment and discouragement.

> *Lean in: Make a plan for daily renewal. Maybe it's simply a commitment to read a scripture or devotional each morning. Find a way to stick to it, whether forty-five seconds, five minutes, whatever you have. Make*

daily renewal (daily time reminding yourself of God's word and promises) a priority, and see how it affects your perspective.

12

FINISH

> *Then David continued, "Be strong and courageous, and do the work. Don't be afraid or discouraged, for the Lord God, my God is with you. He will not fail you or forsake you. He will see to it that all the work related to the Temple of the Lord is finished correctly."*
>
> —*1 Chronicles 28:20 (NLT)*

I've been familiar for years with the multiple appearances of "Be strong and courageous" in the Bible. I've heard sermons on the many times and various situations in which God commands, "Be strong and courageous." Joshua received this emphatic commission before embarking on his epic adventures. King Hezekiah used it in his speech delivered to the people of Jerusalem on the eve of invasion by the Assyrians. But only recently did I discover this instance where the period isn't after courageous; it's after "and do the work." We don't often associate courage with working. But here it is in the context of finishing a lengthy and tedious project. Boy, does that fit the special mom's job description. It's not enough to be courageous at the doctor appointment, during the meltdown or crisis, at the IEP meeting, or during hospital stay. The truth is that courage is required to continue the work to its completion every single day—forever. I love that in the NIV version above, David follows up with, "Don't be afraid or discouraged, for the Lord God, my God, is with you." In this, a father is encouraging his son to complete a monumental project that will span his entire lifetime and define the lives and talents of the entire generation of Israelites. Dad admonishes his son to be courageous, not by saying, "I'll be here by your side," but by saying, "God—*my God*—is with you."

How can you defeat the discouragement or fear that can seep into your heart after long days and longer nights? Know that the Lord God—who is *the* God—is with you. He goes before you; he doesn't leave you alone. He will not fail or forsake you. And *he* will see to it that all the work related to your project is finished correctly. Meditate on the privilege and honor that he has ordained a specific plan and course for you, and he promises to enable you to do the work.

> *Lean in: Rest in the fact that God knows your "job" and that it's not easy and sometimes not fun. Ask for renewed strength, for an overflow of the Holy Spirit's presence, which will enable you to do the work joyfully and completely. Envision the great satisfaction of finishing what you were created to do.*

13

PRAISE

*Why, my soul, are you downcast? Why so
disturbed within me? Put your hope in God, for I
will yet praise him, my Savior and my God.*

—Psalms 43:5 (NIV)

Praise. I could've listed hundreds of scripture references, rather than one, for today's devotional. Think of praise like a key. It is *the* key. It will unlock whatever is locked up. If there is one lesson I've learned above all else in my journey, it is that giving praise to God changes things. Not figuratively, but quite literally. Throughout the Old and New Testaments of the Bible, there are stories of walls literally crumbling, prison chains actually being broken, when God's people do nothing more than praise him. Audible words of praise from my mouth have undeniable impact on whatever atmosphere or situation I find myself in.

I can look back on so many desperate moments when I had just enough presence of mind to simply praise. I have vivid recollections of sitting inside dark, oppressive MRI rooms, watching my baby's body being mechanically slid in and out of that ominous tube, with my headphones in my ears and Hillsong music being digitally slid into my mind and spirit. In times that could have been the lowest, I distinctly remember the undeniable presence of God with me. His comforting embrace was so warm and real, protecting my heart and mind, and reassuring me that his love for me and his plans to prosper my family were sincere and secure.

During moments of frustration or anger, by forcing praise through my mind and out of my mouth, I have been able to emerge to a place of peace and calm, like emerging from a tempest or flood that would otherwise drown me completely. Very similar to the prisoners whose chains were broken in Acts 16, I have felt my arms come loose from whatever was holding me down and reach instinctively upward as I praised through a battle in my mind, my home, my marriage, and my finances. Years ago I read the book *The Purpose Driven Life*, in which Rick Warren unveils the true, deepest, most basic purpose for which we were all created: to bring glory to God. Praise, he proposes, is intrinsic to our innermost being. When we praise, we change things from the inside out.

Although essential to our fulfillment, praise often does not feel natural. When all hell breaks loose, for example, praise does not seem the appropriate response. When all hope is lost, dreams are dashed, or devastation strikes, praise is not the first thing to come out of our mouths. However, it is the one thing that will cause the tide to turn, both within our own hearts and minds as well as in the atmosphere and circumstances we are facing.

> *Lean in: Determine to give praise to God today. Do it first in your heart and mind, but at some point, do it with your voice. Announce to the air around you that your God is great and mighty and worthy to be praised. That he is awesome, powerful, and in control of everything. That every situation, illness, and circumstance must bow to his sovereignty. I promise that you will feel differently than when you started.*

14

CHOOSE

You knit me together in my mother's womb. I praise you because I am fearfully and wonderfully made.

—Psalms 139:13b, 14a (NIV)

When you receive a diagnosis for your child, it is usually in the form of medical reports. The full doctor's report gets sent home with you, along with plenty of supporting documentation. In our case, the geneticist sent us home with medical journal reports that outlined all the possible (terrible) characteristics or symptoms that would accompany our son's genetic anomaly. He was just an infant, but the reports painted a bleak outlook for his future.

Our choice that day, and every day since for the past sixteen years, was: upon which report would we base our lives?

We could treat this infant as if he were already a disabled person, who would be defined by the limits and difficulties described in the reports. Or we could believe the report in Psalm 127 that says children are an inheritance of the Lord. And the report in Psalm 139 says that he has knit us together in our mother's womb, and we are fearfully and wonderfully made—all of us.

I'm not talking about being delusional or living in a state of denial. We are aware of the challenges that our little guy faced—and still faces. But we have taken our example from the book of Numbers, when Moses sent out twelve spies to report on the land the God had promised them. Ten of them came back with a really negative report about the challenges to be faced. But two of the spies saw beyond challenges. All twelve agreed it was a land better than any they had seen before with wonderful fruit. But only two spies understood that all the blessings and treasures were completely worth the price of a few obstacles. Further, they insisted, the Lord would surely help them overcome. Unfortunately the masses went with the ten spies, fearing the battle that would be required for such a wonderful prize.

So we base our lives on God's promises—his report. Just as in the example of the Israelite spies, the prize has certainly been worth the battles. Yes, battles there have been aplenty. But the reward, the treasure, and the Promised Land are exactly as reported! Our son may have similarities to the original medical reports, but if I'm being honest he is much more accurately described by those psalms. It's a choice we make every day, and in the face of every set back and situation. We are just one choice away from a really good report! Won't that be nice for a change?

> *Lean in: Ask God to show you his report. Dig into the Bible and read what he says about our lives and our purpose. That report applies to your child as well. He will begin to reveal the "milk and honey" within your current circumstance as you put greater trust in his promises and less emphasis on the reports given to you by others.*

ABOUT THE AUTHOR

Married for twenty-four years with two teenage sons, Melanie Gomez's passion is to share the message with every special-needs mom that there is joy, there is purpose, and there is hope in their journey.

With a master's degree and years of experience in the corporate world, Melanie now finds herself an expert in the nontraditional areas of caregiving, homeschooling, juggling multiple social and therapeutic schedules, chauffeuring, and cheerleading for her family.

Melanie; her husband, Tony; and their boys, Ben and Nick, recently moved from Chicago back to their native Florida, where they are looking forward to sunshine and flip-flops all year long.

Made in the USA
Monee, IL
28 September 2023

43636186R00039